FACE PAINTIN

Why does the fire salamander have so many flashy spots? Because he wants other animals to believe that he is dangerous. Many animals use vibrant colors for protection. Some may threaten their enemies with big painted eyes – at the tip of their tail! Others rely on camouflage colors so that no one will detect them. What about the rooster? He just wants to be beautiful!

F or thousands of years people have used brushes, sponges or their own fingers to paint their faces with dynamic colors. For instance, war paint is used to frighten enemies. Also, face paint is used for looking festive at celebrations and ceremonies. Moreover, people paint their faces in funny ways to make others laugh.

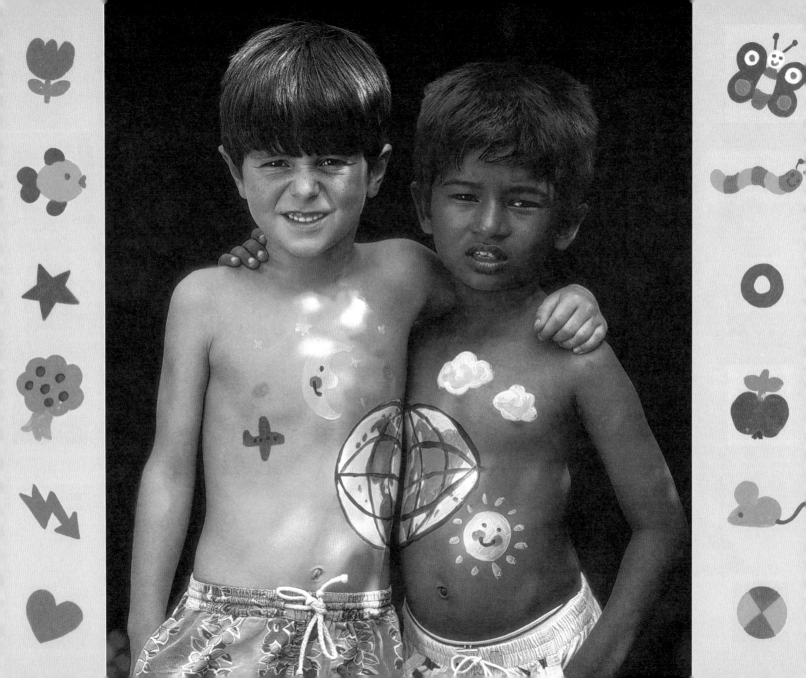

FACE PAINTING

Original text:
Clemens Creynfeld
and
Günther Frorath

Make-up:
Frantisek Machác,
Jürgen Pankarz
and
Elisabeth Kunath

Photographs:
Paul Maaßen

Illustrations:
Jürgen Pankarz

MUD PUDDLE BOOKS, INC.
New York, New York

Of course, nobody wants to read a boring

introduction. Instead, everyone wants to quickly take the brush

and face paint and look like  a pirate, a vampire

or a fairy  right away.

But, wait! These first few pages are very important and will help you make the most of your face painting fun. Here, we will explain you what to do with the colors and what else you need.

For starters try painting small blots on the back of your hand, for example a sun or a flower. These you can paint yourself. But, of course, as we progress, you'll find it's more fun to have somebody join you. You can ask your mom to turn you into a cat, or you can paint a clown's nose for a friend.

What you need

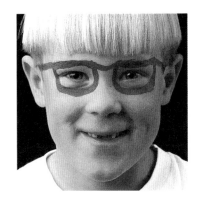

One of the best things about this book is that it comes in a kit that already includes the face paint and brush.

If you wish to paint a large surface (for instance, the white foundation of a clown's face) it is best to use a small sponge. Maybe your mom has one that she uses for her cosmetics. Other sponges would work just as well. If you only have a big sponge, you can always take scissors and cut it into smaller pieces.

Now, all you need is water. Fill one bowl (for the sponge) and one or two glasses (for the brush).

Cotton swabs are also very helpful. They can be used for applying face paint as well as for wiping it off or for correcting mistakes.

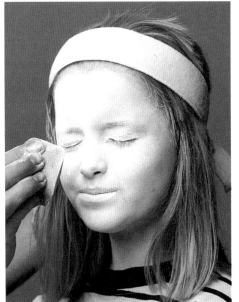

The enclosed face paint is nontoxic and doesn't stain (it is easily removed by using soap and

water). Still, it would probably be best if you put on an old shirt before using the paint.
Also, anything that can be used for cleaning and washing is useful: paper towels, rags or towels.

Have a small mirror handy. You are about to get started!

Getting started

Using your fingers

If you dampen the paint and touch it with your fingers, you will quickly find out how much paint you need to apply to make the color look vibrant or how much you need to water it down to make the color appear soft. Test this by painting big red spots with your fingers.

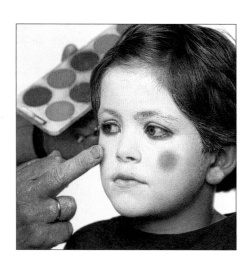

Using a sponge

Simply wet the sponge and squeeze out the liquid until it's merely damp. Then, rub it in the paint and dab it on the face.

You can also smear instead of dabbing it on. It's faster, but it will leave streaks. These can look funny, too. You can always dab it afterwards.

Face painting is easiest when you use both fingers and sponges. For example, see the Native American faces on pages 26 and 27. First, using a sponge, wipe the whole face with color. Once the paint has dried, add the war paint with your fingers.

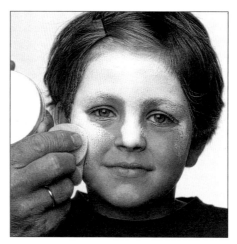

Using a brush

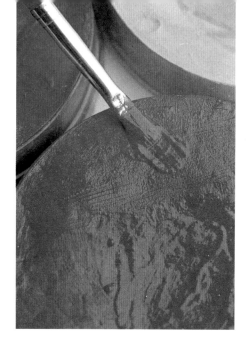

Take the brush, dip it in the water and stir the color of your choice (let's say red). Circle the brush as if you were stirring a cup of hot chocolate. If you need more liquid dip the brush again in the water.

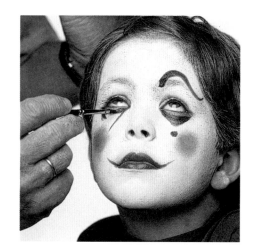

Face painting is fun
And looks great when you're done!

Now, try to paint the shape of a heart on your friend's cheek. It doesn't matter if you slip or if the shape isn't perfect. Just dampen a cotton swap and circle it until the paint is removed.

By the way, you might want to paint other shapes or patterns using different colors. Just make sure that the brush is clean.

Remember to always rinse out the brush when you're finished with a color. When you rinse the brush, make sure that the water is clear. Otherwise the colors will not look as vibrant.

The next steps

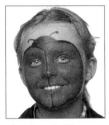

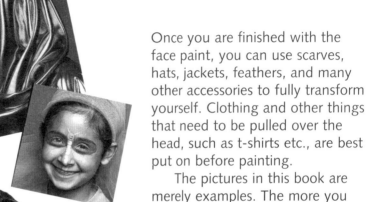

Once you have learned how to paint simple shapes, such as hearts, you will want to start painting your face, perhaps like a ladybug or a wild tiger.

To do so you will have to paint the entire face. The primary color, such as the tiger's yellow, is best applied by using a small sponge. First, dip the sponge into the water until it is fully wet. Then, squeeze the water out, leaving the sponge damp. Next, absorb the paint and dab it carefully all over the face until you have created an even surface.

After completing the primary layer you can start working on the details. To make it easier for yourself, rest your "painting hand" on your other hand.

Once you are finished with the face paint, you can use scarves, hats, jackets, feathers, and many other accessories to fully transform yourself. Clothing and other things that need to be pulled over the head, such as t-shirts etc., are best put on before painting.

The pictures in this book are merely examples. The more you use your own imagination the better your painted face or masquerade will turn out.

13

To avoid shaking, support the hand that does the painting.

14

How to mix colors

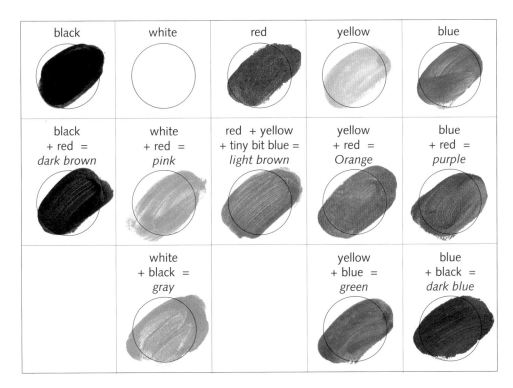

black	white	red	yellow	blue
black + red = *dark brown*	white + red = *pink*	red + yellow + tiny bit blue = *light brown*	yellow + red = *Orange*	blue + red = *purple*
	white + black = *gray*		yellow + blue = *green*	blue + black = *dark blue*

Your kit contains five colors, which can easily be mixed. This chart shows you what happens when you, for example, mix red and blue: purple.

You can mix colors either on your hand or you can create a palette for mixing colors (use, for example, the inside of the top of a plastic container or the cardboard from a laundered shirt). Afterwards, clean the paint container with a damp sponge.

Important:
Mixing with black creates a darker tone.
Mixing with white creates a lighter tone (except red + white = pink). Certainly, there are further color combinations possible. See what you can create yourself.

SMALL FACEPAINTINGS

POP QUIZ!!! No, just kidding. But, did you read the previous pages thoroughly? Great! (But don't worry: there are no mistakes in face painting, anyway!) In order to make these small face paintings you need a "model". The model could be a friend who is willing to sit still or someone who would like to have a birthday cake painted on her cheeks. Then again, maybe someone wants you to be the model.

STAYING STILL

!
.

Birthdays come once a year.
Tho' you wish they were always here.
You're surrounded by family and friends,
Everyone who holds you dear.

Plump & ripe,
they grow on trees
Where the wind
sways their leaves.

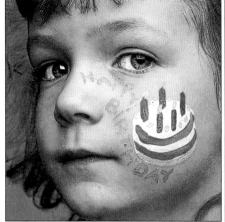

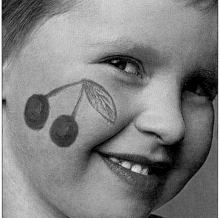

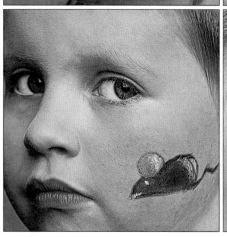

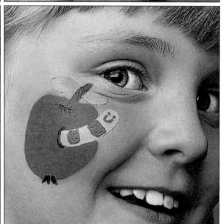

There's a mouse
In my house!
(Be nice
To mice!)

Worm, go way,
That apple is mine.
Unless you want to stay
And play!

Panda bear.

Penguin

You can draw them on your face:

It's easy!

18

19

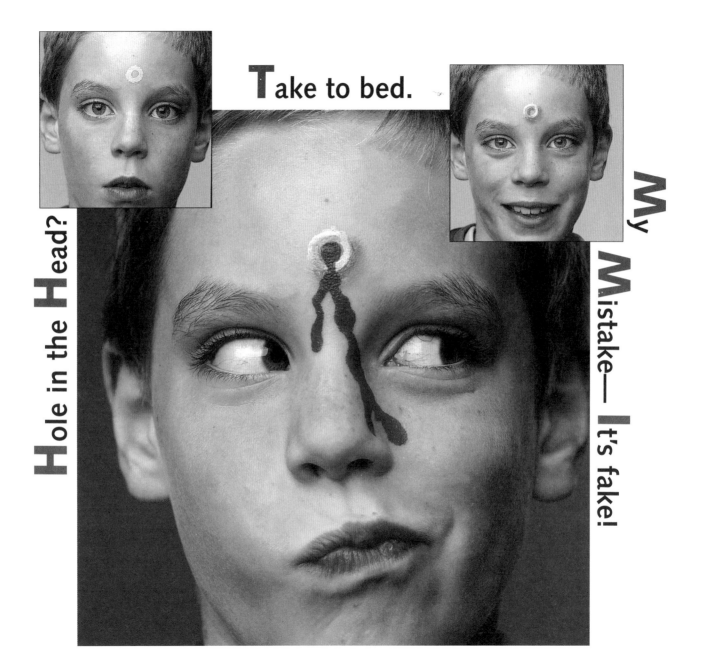

Hole in the Head?

Take to bed.

My Mistake— It's fake!

20

Tattoos

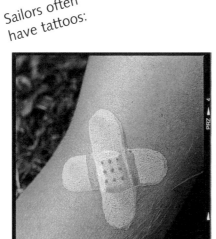

Sailors often have tattoos:

For example an anchor on an arm

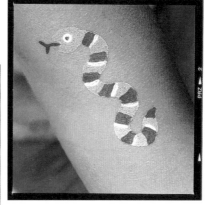

Or a rose, or a dragon. Or…

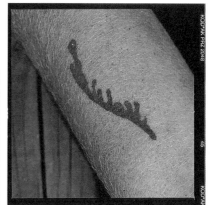

Tattoos

Butterfly

You have two eyes and a nose. The butterfly has two wings and a body.

Start like this: Draw the outline (also called the contours) of the butterfly's body and wings. Then, select and mix the most beautiful colors and fill in the area.

As long as the paint is wet, the base color can be changed – for example, you can shade a white face by using a little blue or green.

Painting the eyes: Press the sponge until you have a pointed tip. Dab the closed eyes with color, starting from the nose outwards. Work carefully. Remember, the paint is nontoxic, so nothing really can happen.

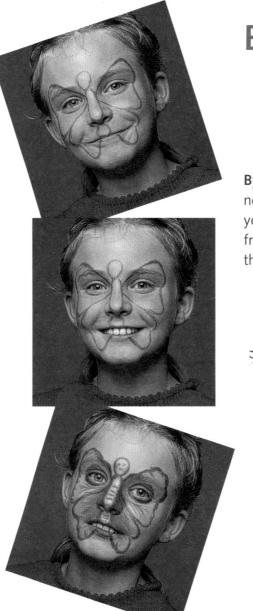

Butterfly

By the way: If you're itching and need to scratch yourself, don't use your fingers. You could smudge the fresh paint. Instead, use the tip of the brush to scratch.

You're as beautiful as a rose
With a carrot for a nose!

It doesn't
take hours
To transform
a face
with
flowers!

How do you paint larger areas, such as beautiful red cheeks (or the whole face)?

It's best done this way: First, dab the face paint. Then, rub it on using circular movements.

Remember: as long as the base color is wet, you can change the shade – for example, add a little blue or green.

THE

WILD

WILD

W
E
S
T

It's **easy** to transform your face into a Native American. Begin by facing a mirror! Using both index fingers, paint stripes on both sides of your face simultaneously. Start in the middle of your face and move outward: go from the nose towards the ears, from the mouth to the chin, and so on.

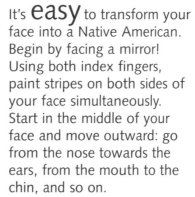

27

A ladybug is easy
And lots of fun to do.

A tiny dot here,
    A tiny dot there,
No bug is as cute as you!

First, draw the outline, then fill in the area. Finally, add the dots (similar to the butterfly).

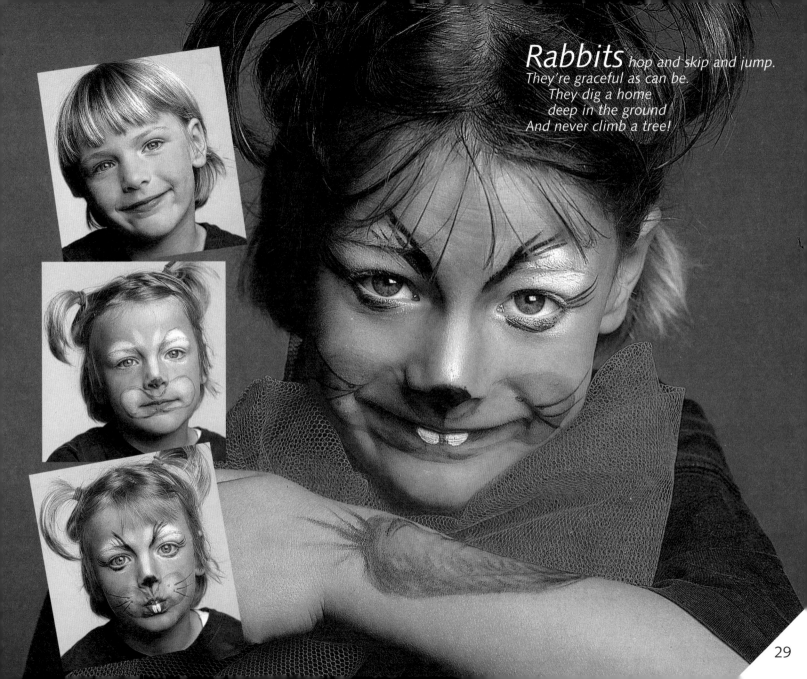

Rabbits hop and skip and jump.
They're graceful as can be.
  They dig a home
    deep in the ground
And never climb a tree!

FUNNY CLOWNS

Not every clown has a red nose. But all of these clowns are funny. It's easy to paint a clown's face. Start with spots on your nose and cheeks. After your face is painted you can transform yourself into a circus clown by wearing crazy hats, colorful bows and oversized shoes.

This pony-tailed **hen** *shops wearing high heels. She's thrifty and smart and finds the best deals.*

The **zebra** *color is a mystery*
Baffling men since the dawn of history.
Is he black with stripes of white
Or is it the other way that's right?

Rabbit, *rabbit, happy all day,*
Won't you come out and play?

A tricky **mouse** *paints a disguise;*
Looks like a cat and feels so wise.

This odd animal,
A **coati** by name,
Easily removes his paint
(You can do the same!)

A happy **hamster**
Through a hoop flies.
He wears tiger stripes
As his disguise.

By painting a pig on a **parrot,**
this owl so wise
Creates a colorful pig that flies.

This dog's a **hot dog** long and really lean
He dresses as a codfish that's blue and green.

What.....is it **already** that late???

To make a really creepy **witch,** paint bushy eyebrows. Use a dark color for your lips and dab red color around your eyes with a sponge. Then, follow the creases in your face with a brush. You can always add creases where there aren't any.

Before you start painting the SKULL, feel your face with both hands. Your face is like a roller coaster. Begin with a white base covering your entire face (be careful around the eyes). Leave the areas that rise (such as your cheekbones and forehead) white. Paint the areas that sink in (such as

the sides of your face where the upper and lower jaws meet) dark.

By the way, you can create a bald-headed look by using a rubber mask or bald pate. You can find these accessories in stores carrying Halloween supplies. Or you can use a bathing cap or hood instead.

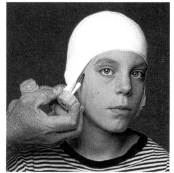
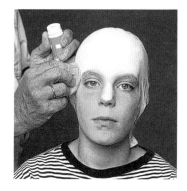

Wild Animals and Vampires

Dracula is his name.
Biting at midnight is his game.

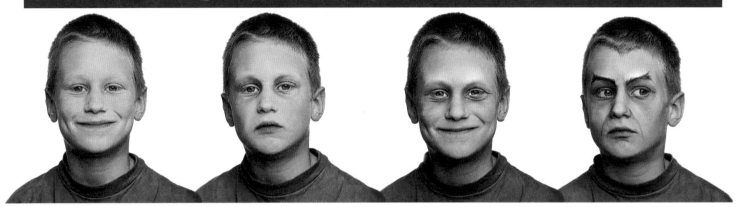

At first you look nice and **funny**. But that changes as you dab away the niceness with a sponge. The area around the eyes turns red **like blood** and your cheeks and forehead turn white like the moon in Transylvania. Then, it's time to paint the eyebrows and lips. And finally, the most important:
the
pointy
teeth.

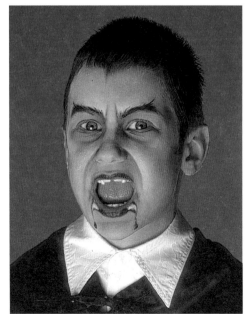

41

ZEbra

42

CObra

Pussy-cat paws, Pussy-cat claws.

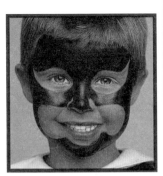
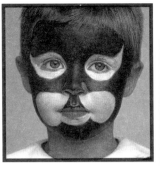

Painted faces turn out especially beautiful if they glitter and glow. You can apply **glitter gel,** on the dried face paint to achieve a shining, shimmering result.

Keep in mind that it's always easier to paint dark colors on light surfaces than light colors on dark surfaces. That's why you should start painting the white area around the mouth and eyes. Then add the yellow for the tiger's face and hair followed by extra white jags at the mouth and eyes. Finally, add the black tiger stripes!

...TIGER!

Riger...

Rooger...

Roger...

Do you want the monkey's ears to stick out? Use modeling clay!

First paint the brown face of the

Monkey

Then, let the dark fur grow on top.

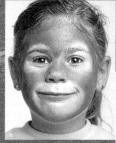

...or this
or
that

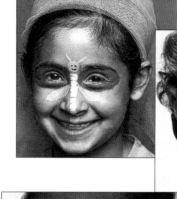

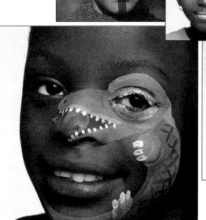

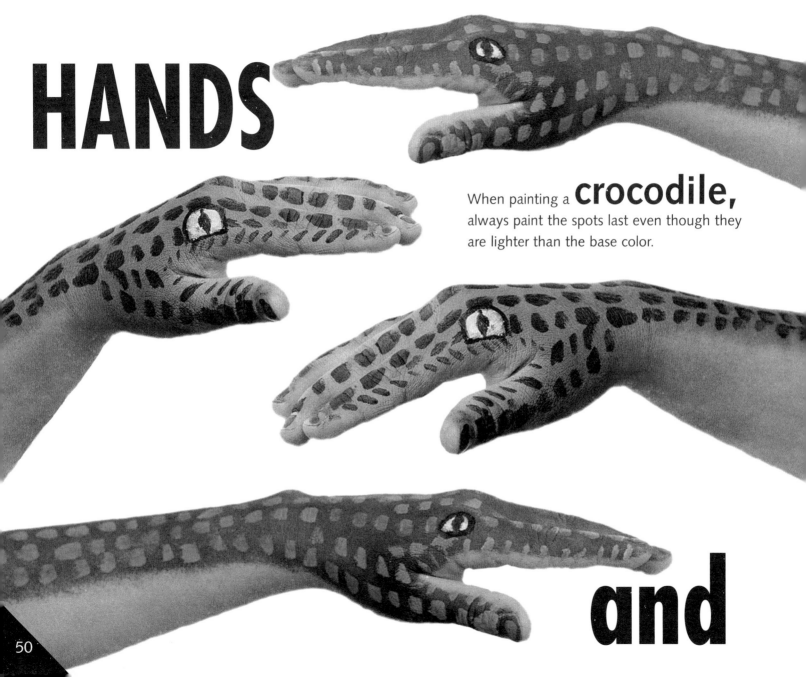

HANDS

When painting a **crocodile,** always paint the spots last even though they are lighter than the base color.

and

FEET

All sorts of elephants!

Sweet feet

53

Colorful

clowns.

Wide-
eyed
owl
at
night!

HO! HO! HO!

A seaman's life for me!

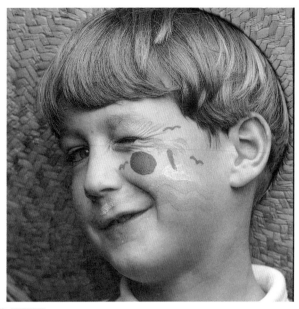

Welcome aboard!

We're having a big party with many pirates and sailors. Buccaneers have sunburnt faces (don't forget neck and ears) and scars from fights.

It's best to dab the stubbly beard on with a porous sponge. "Blood paint" is available in tubes in stores that carry Halloween supplies.

Captain Hook

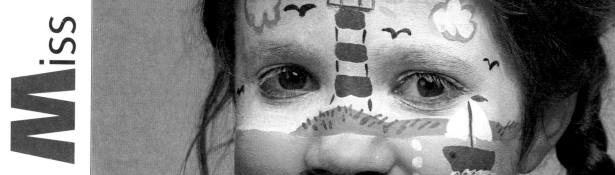

Miss

Captain

WEATHER FERRY

59

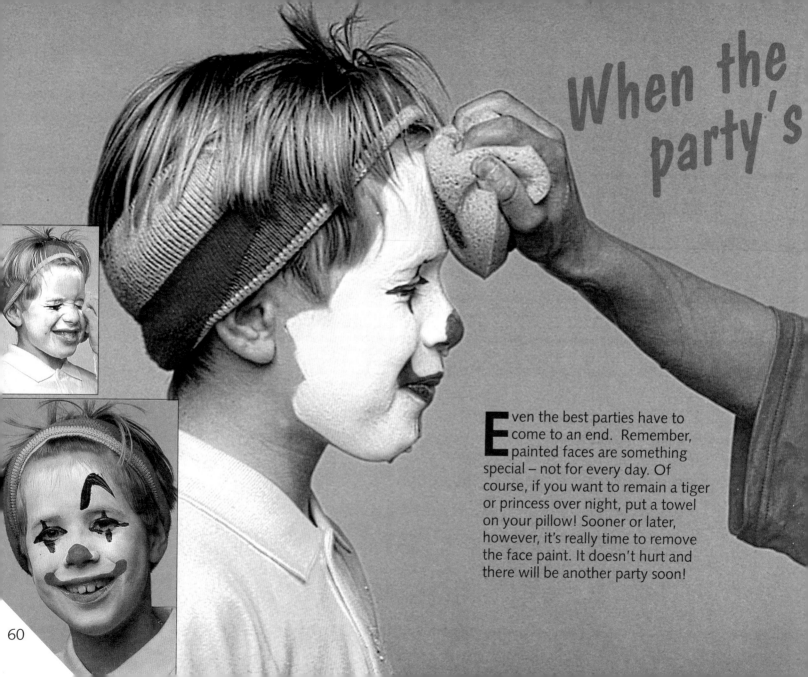

Even the best parties have to come to an end. Remember, painted faces are something special – not for every day. Of course, if you want to remain a tiger or princess over night, put a towel on your pillow! Sooner or later, however, it's really time to remove the face paint. It doesn't hurt and there will be another party soon!

60

over...

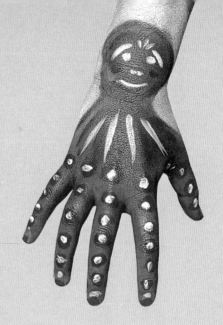

Face Painting

ISBN: 1-59412-042-0

Published by Mud Puddle Books, Inc.
54 West 21st Street, Suite 601,
New York, NY 10010
info@mudpuddlebooks.com

Printed in China.

10 9 8 7 6 5 4 3 2

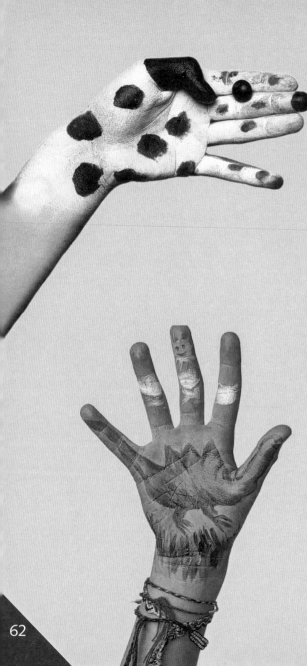

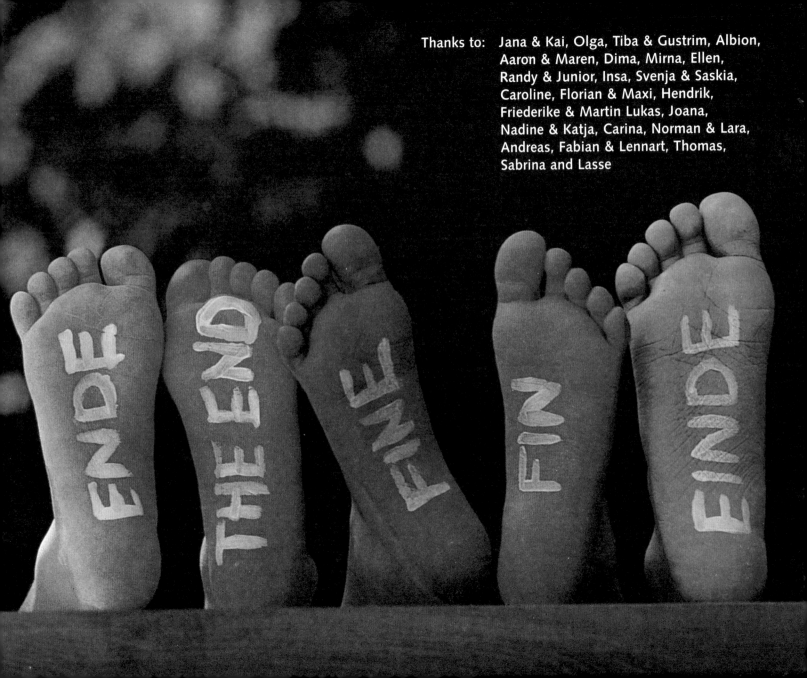

Thanks to: Jana & Kai, Olga, Tiba & Gustrim, Albion,
Aaron & Maren, Dima, Mirna, Ellen,
Randy & Junior, Insa, Svenja & Saskia,
Caroline, Florian & Maxi, Hendrik,
Friederike & Martin Lukas, Joana,
Nadine & Katja, Carina, Norman & Lara,
Andreas, Fabian & Lennart, Thomas,
Sabrina and Lasse

MUD PUDDLE BOOKS, INC.
New York, New York